Lost Underground

Robert Gott

Illustrated by Carol Pelham-Thorman

Rigby

Lost Underground

Rigby Heinemann
a division of Reed International Books Australia Pty Ltd
22 Salmon Street, Port Melbourne, Victoria 3207
World Wide Web http://www.rigby.com.au
Email info@hi.com.au

Offices in Sydney, Brisbane, Perth and Adelaide. Associated companies, branches and representatives throughout the world.

2005 2004 2003 2002 2001
10 9 8 7 6 5 4 3 2 1

Text by Robert Gott
Illustrated by Carol Pelham-Thorman
Designed by Andrew Cunningham

Typeset in Galliard
Printed by Impact Printing

National Library of Australia
ISBN 0 7312 3241 0

Contents

Chapter One

Camping

"But he'll ruin everything. He's just a menace."

Eleven-year-old Louisa Mackenzie was reacting to the news that her ten-year-old cousin, Marcus, was coming with them on their camping trip. Louisa's brother Declan, who was the same age as Marcus, agreed with her.

"Why, Dad?" he asked. "Why does he have to come? He'll wreck everything."

Mr Mackenzie laughed.

"Oh, come on. He's not that bad."

Declan and Louisa looked at each other. They knew just how bad Marcus could be.

"Your Aunt Cindy needs a break. I can't say no to my sister, can I?"

Louisa and Declan had been looking forward to this camping trip. Their mother had gone interstate on business and their father had decided to surprise her by driving up to meet her.

"That way she won't be so disappointed about having to spend her birthday away from home," he had said. Along the way, they were going to camp. Neither Louisa nor Declan had ever been camping before.

Marcus arrived the night before the trip was due to begin. A few minutes before dinner, he was nowhere to be found.

"Marcus!" called Mr Mackenzie.

"You're wasting your time," said Louisa. " He never ever answers when you call him."

"Marcus!" Mr Mackenzie called again and this time he was annoyed.

"He's probably outside somewhere," said Declan. "Lucky there aren't any rivers near here," he added, so quietly that only Louisa heard him. She laughed.

"What are you two laughing at?" asked Mr Mackenzie.

"Nothing," she said. "Private joke."

"Well, I'm not going to wait any longer," said Mr Mackenzie. "I'll serve up dinner without him and his can just get cold."

Marcus had a mysterious radar that always drew him back just as hot food hit the table.

"Where have you been?" asked Mr Mackenzie crossly. "I called and called."

Marcus didn't say anything. He just

smiled at his uncle and began eating. Mr Mackenzie began to think that perhaps Marcus might be a handful after all.

"What's that?" Marcus asked and pointed to a colourful beetle pinned to a board in Louisa's room. There were lots of other beetles pinned to the board as well, but the one Marcus was pointing to was the biggest and the most colourful.

"It's a goliath beetle," said Louisa. She was trying to be polite but Marcus had already asked her a dozen questions about her insect collection and she was sick of answering him.

"How can you like insects?" he asked, turning up his nose in disgust.

"I like spiders best of all," said Louisa, "and I've got a huge, live tarantula in my drawer. Do you want to hold it?"

Marcus looked shocked.

"I don't believe you," he said.

"Is that so?" she asked, quietly.

Louisa opened the drawer slowly saying, "Hello Harry" as she did so. She reached in and pretended to scoop up the imaginary spider. When she turned around, Marcus had fled.

The next morning, when the car was packed and breakfast eaten, Marcus and the Mackenzies set out.

"Your mother will love this surprise," said Mr Mackenzie. "It's the best birthday present she could have."

"What's Aunt Helen doing?" asked Marcus.

"She's a lawyer," said Declan. "She's working on a case."

Marcus was looking out the window and not listening to the reply. He did that a lot—asked a question but didn't bother to listen to the answer.

The houses gradually gave way to fields and orchards and then to forest. Soon, they had left the city far behind them.

Marcus played an electronic game. The blips and bleeps drove everyone crazy, but Marcus said that there wasn't any point playing it with the sound turned off. Soon though, he began to feel sick.

"I'm carsick," he said.

"Wind down the window," said Mr Mackenzie. He understood now why his sister needed a break from Marcus.

"I'm bored," said Marcus.

"I'm hungry," said Marcus.

"I'm thirsty," said Marcus.

"Are we there yet?" asked Marcus.

Just before sunset, Mr Mackenzie pulled off the road into a clearing. They managed to get their tents up and a fire started before darkness fell.

Mr Mackenzie had a one-person tent and Louisa, Declan and Marcus were to share a two-person tent. There was easily enough room in it for three children. Mr Mackenzie cooked a meal of baked beans

and sausages, then they sat around the fire watching the sparks fly upwards.

"Now listen carefully," said Mr Mackenzie. Declan stared at his father's face watching the way the firelight played on it. Declan thought he looked a bit scary. It reminded him of how you could make a scary face by holding a torch under your chin.

"No-one," said his father, "is to go wandering off. I don't know what the countryside is like around here. There could be holes or ditches or fallen branches. I don't want anybody getting hurt. We'll all go exploring together in the morning. That means you especially, Marcus. You're not to go outside the area of firelight."

Marcus said nothing, because Marcus wasn't there.

"Are you listening to me? Marcus?"

Mr Mackenzie suddenly realised that Marcus had slipped away soon after the meal. He stood up.

"Marcus!" he roared at the top of his voice. Louisa hoped that the animals that lived around the clearing hadn't gone to sleep yet, because if they had, they'd be awake again now.

Mr Mackenzie put his hands on his hips and said, "How can someone so small be so annoying?"

Declan and Louisa laughed.

"You're not the first person to ask that," said Declan.

"I'll have to find him," said Mr Mackenzie. "You two stay here."

Louisa and Declan knew their father was angry. He went to his tent and returned with a torch.

"He can't be far away," he said. "I won't be long."

Mr Mackenzie disappeared into the surrounding darkness, calling Marcus's name as he went.

Soon his voice faded and the glimmer of his torch passed from view. The only sounds now were the crackling of the fire and the rustling of the leaves in the trees.

"I knew this would happen," said Declan.

"Gotcha!" said Louisa as she scooped yet another bug into her specimen jar.

"It sure is dark," said Declan.

Louisa thought she heard a hint of nervousness in his voice.

"It sure is," she said and smiled to herself. Louisa waited a moment, then jumped up suddenly.

"What was that?" she asked anxiously.

"What?" said Declan, alert.

"Shhh. That noise."

"There's no noise. You're just trying to scare me," said Declan.

"I heard something. Something big."

Chapter Two
A Fall

Louisa hadn't heard any unusual noise, but she knew that Declan was now primed to hear a scary story.

"Shhh," she said again. "It might be the madman."

"What are you talking about? There's no madman," said Declan. One part of him knew that Louisa was just trying to frighten him; another part felt like she was succeeding.

"In the woods around here," she said, her voice low, "there's a madman.

He lives alone and they say he carries a big stick wherever he goes. He's always out in the woods and he scares everyone. They reckon that anyone who comes near where he lives gets whacked with the stick. Yep, that's what people say."

As she was saying this, the wind began to rise and the swaying trees cast large shadows that lurched from side to side. Branches began to clatter against one another. An owl hooted and somewhere

in the darkness an animal stirred and skittered over dead leaves.

"Hear that?" said Louisa, her voice deliberately tight. "He's over there!"

She had barely finished this sentence when a loud crash startled them. Each child was now as frightened as the other. Louisa had managed to scare them both.

"Dad?" called Declan.

There was no answer.

"Is it the madman?" asked Declan. His voice was shaky. He sounded as if he was close to tears.

"Don't be silly," said Louisa, feeling guilty about upsetting her brother. She was also feeling silly that she was very scared herself. "There is no madman. It's just a story I made up."

"Well, what is it then?" Declan did not sound convinced.

"We'll go and see," she said, trying desperately to sound brave.

"Dad said not to move," said Declan.

He remembered he had once read something about monsters never coming too close to a fire.

But Declan didn't want to stay on his own, even if it was near the fire, so he reluctantly joined Louisa as she tip-toed toward the site of the crash. It seemed ridiculous to tip-toe in the middle of a forest but it also seemed like the natural thing to do.

"It was just over there," Louisa said. "Near the tents. Come on." Louisa quickly ducked inside and fetched a torch for each of them. They switched them on and swept the ground behind the tents.

At first they saw nothing unusual, but then, in the distance, Louisa spotted what had made the crash that had so unnerved them. A branch, its end newly broken, lay on the ground. The wind must have brought it down.

"That's all it was," said Louisa. She felt more relief than she was willing to

admit to. But her relief didn't last long. A cry of "Help! Over here! Help!" cut through the night air.

"That's Marcus," said Declan.

They listened for his voice again. It was hard with the wind blowing to work out where the voice was coming from.

"Help!" he called again.

"That way!" said Louisa. She and Declan forgot what their father had said.

They hurried towards the voice pushing their way through undergrowth and low-growing branches. The light from their torches bounced around as they moved as quickly as they could.

"Help!" There it was again. And this time much closer. They were almost upon him. They reached a place where the ground fell away into a kind of ditch.

"Help!" Marcus's voice was coming from the bottom of the ditch.

"Are you all right?" called Louisa.

"Yes," he said. "It's too slippery to get back up, that's all. I fell," he added unnecessarily.

Declan shone his torch over the edge of the ditch and found Marcus. It was quite a long way down. He was standing at the bottom looking up at them, his hand shielding his eyes from the glare of the torch. The walls of the ditch were sweaty with mud. They could see where Marcus had tried to scramble up and

where he had slipped back again. He was covered in mud.

"We'll have to get Dad," said Louisa.

From behind her, Mr Mackenzie said, "That won't be necessary. I'm here."

She jumped. She hadn't heard him approaching.

"I'll talk to you two later," he said. "I asked you to stay near the fire. At the moment, though, I've got to figure out a way of getting your cousin out of there."

The only solution seemed to be to slide down into the ditch and hope that his walking shoes had enough grip to allow him to carry Marcus back up again.

Mr Mackenzie began his descent carefully. He soon realised that he needed both hands free to guide him. He threw his torch down and told Marcus to shine it where he was putting his feet so he could see any obstacles. Marcus did, for a few seconds, then he shone it around the ditch.

He couldn't have chosen a worse moment to take the beam off his uncle's feet. Mr Mackenzie put his foot down on a loose rock and the rock gave way. His ankle turned painfully and he slid helplessly into the ditch.

He landed almost exactly where Marcus was standing. He was covered in mud and his ankle was beginning to throb. Marcus shone the torch into Mr Mackenzie's face, but when he saw the look on that face he turned the torch off.

"Is everything all right?" Louisa called from the edge of the ditch.

"Yes," said her father through gritted teeth. "Everything is perfectly fine."

Luckily, Mr Mackenzie's shoes proved to have excellent grip and he was able to bring Marcus up out of the ditch safely.

But every time Mr Mackenzie put his foot down, he felt a sharp stab of pain. He didn't think he'd broken his ankle, but he was sure he'd sprained it badly. He had no choice though. He had to put weight on it in order to climb from the ditch.

Mr Mackenzie limped back to camp with the children following. Louisa and Declan were expecting a lecture about disobeying his orders, but Mr Mackenzie was in such a bad mood that he simply told them to go straight to bed and he then went into his tent. His tone of voice made any suggestion that it was too early for bed, out of the question.

Once they were in their sleeping bags, Louisa told Marcus that he was an idiot. She spoke in a low voice so that her father, whose tent was close by, couldn't hear her. She wanted to say that he was ruining their holiday, but she thought that might be a bit mean.

"It wasn't my fault," said Marcus. "I was chased by a...um...a...a tiger. Yes, I was chased by this huge tiger."

"There are no tigers here, Marcus. They live in India and Siberia."

"It must have escaped from a circus," said Marcus.

"There are no circuses around here," said Declan.

"Good night, Marcus," said Louisa firmly.

Chapter Three

The Storm

The next morning, the children woke early. Marcus was still caked with mud from the night before and he'd smeared it all over his sleeping bag, too.

Mr Mackenzie crawled out of his tent. He'd towelled a lot of the mud off his face and hands, but his clothes were filthy. Louisa expected him to have a face like thunder, but instead it was twisted with pain.

"My ankle's pretty bad," he said. He managed to sit in a fold-away chair and

Louisa and Declan helped him raise his foot and rest it on a second fold-away chair. His ankle had swollen to almost twice its usual size and it was purple.

"Is it broken?" asked Marcus, his eyes were wide with excitement. He'd never seen a broken ankle before.

"No, Marcus. It's just a bad sprain." He turned to Louisa. "I don't think I can walk on it or drive the car."

"It should have been strapped up," said Louisa. "And you should have put ice on it last night."

"Where are we going to get ice out here," said Declan reasonably.

"There's ice in the cooler," said Louisa.

"It would have melted by now," said Declan.

"It would still have been cold last night," said Louisa.

"All right, all right," said Mr Mackenzie. "Let's not have an argument about ice, okay? Louisa, did they teach you how to strap up an ankle in your first-aid course?"

"Yes," she said proudly.

"Well, there's a first-aid kit in the car. It'll have bandages in it," said Mr Mackenzie.

Louisa strapped up her father's ankle neatly. Marcus watched, fascinated, as if he was watching a delicate operation.

"That's a very professional job," said Mr Mackenzie.

She blushed at his compliment.

They all pitched in to prepare breakfast, even Marcus, who realised that he was to blame for his uncle's swollen ankle. He thought it might be a good idea to do something right.

In daylight, the place where they had camped wasn't nearly as scary as it had seemed the night before. Mr Mackenzie said that they could go off exploring, so long as they promised to remain within calling distance.

"And you're not to split up," he said. "Marcus, if you head off on your own, you'll wish you were still at the bottom of that ditch. Understand?"

"Yes, Dad. What time are we leaving?" asked Declan.

"I think we'll have to stay here for another night," said Mr Mackenzie. "By tomorrow, I should be able to drive."

Soon after the children had set out, the sun went behind the clouds and the smell of rain drifted on the wind. The sky turned grey and then dark blue and then black. Lightning played across the sky, but it was so far away that only the faintest sound of thunder followed.

Mr Mackenzie called out. "Louisa! Declan! Marcus!"

He was worried about the approaching storm. It looked severe.

The children heard Mr Mackenzie calling. After last night, they were not tempted to ignore him. They hurried back to camp.

"We found a cave," said Declan. "It's huge. At least we think it's huge. We couldn't see anything because we didn't have our torches."

The wind rose like a fist and punched its way through the camp. It was quickly followed by a white flash of lightning and a deafening clap of thunder. The storm had reached them far sooner than Mr Mackenzie thought it would. The rain began to fall in large, slow drops, but it increased rapidly to the point where it tumbled down so violently that they were soaked within seconds. They could barely hear each other over the rain and wind.

"We can't stay here!" shouted Mr Mackenzie. He had heard that branch crash to the ground last night. This was not a safe place and the lightning that was exploding around them posed a serious threat.

"Get the torches," he yelled, "and show me where the cave is."

Mr Mackenzie, supported by Louisa and Declan, hopped awkwardly towards the entrance of the cave. It was quite small, like a mouth that was slightly open.

But when they squeezed through it and turned on the torches, they found they were in a huge cavern. The pounding of the rain was barely audible in here.

"Stay close to the entrance," Mr Mackenzie said. He shone his torch around the space. Its light caught crystals on the ceiling and on the walls.

"It looks harmless enough," he said. "At least it's out of the storm."

"Look over there," said Declan. His torch had illuminated a wall with paintings on it. There were figures with spears, chasing animals and other marks that looked like handprints. There were also strange figures that weren't human. The wall was crowded with figures.

"Wow," said Mr Mackenzie. "They might be thousands of years old.

"Can we get closer?" asked Louisa. "Can we explore a bit?"

"All right," said Mr Mackenzie, "but stay where I can see you. I want you to be able to see me at all times."

Louisa, Declan and Marcus each had a torch. There were only three torches, so Mr Mackenzie was without one.

The children moved away from the entrance and began following the wall. They kept close to it and Mr Mackenzie could see three beams of torchlight. One beam moved ahead of the others. That was bound to be Marcus, he thought.

He watched as it drew further ahead and within the blink of an eye, it had vanished.

"Marcus!" he called, and his voice echoed wildly. "Marcus!"

The remaining two beams of light came towards him in a hurry.

"What's the matter?" asked Louisa.

"Where's Marcus?"

"Oh, not again," groaned Declan.

Mr Mackenzie struggled to his feet, but he couldn't possibly walk. His ankle had become even more painful. He felt a sudden wave of nausea that made him almost faint.

"What if he's fallen down a hole. It would be just like Marcus," said Louisa.

Mr Mackenzie, trying not to panic, said, "The important thing now is not to panic."

"Don't worry, Dad. Declan and I will find him," said Louisa.

Mr Mackenzie had no choice. His children would have to go after Marcus.

"All right. I'm not happy about this, but there's just no other way," he said.

"You absolutely must stay together at all times and I mean together. I want you to be able to reach out and touch each other at all times. Do you understand? I want you to call out regularly so that I know where you are at all times. Is that clear?"

"Yes," said Louisa.

"Now, let me check your torches, before you go."

As soon as Louisa and Declan had left their father, Declan confessed that he was afraid of the dark and that he wasn't too keen on enclosed spaces.

"Oh great," said Louisa. "You decide to tell me you've got claustrophobia when we're in a cave."

"I didn't say that. I said I didn't like enclosed spaces."

"That is claustrophobia," said Louisa, impatiently. "Go back if you want to."

"I'm not chicken," he said.

"Good. We'll head for where we last saw his torch," she said and then called out, "Dad! We're over here and we're fine!"

"Okay," he replied. He had a dreadful feeling that things were not okay and that something awful was about to happen.

Chapter Four

Into the Cave

"We're still here!" Louisa called.

"Okay," called her father, but this time his voice seemed very far away. Declan didn't think they had gone very far, but when they looked back the light from the entrance had shrunk to a pinhole. They walked a little further and it went out completely. Louisa called again and her voice bounced around the cavern like a ping-pong ball. She thought she heard a reply, but she couldn't be sure.

Beyond the light thrown by the torches, the darkness was absolute. It was so thick, it almost seemed solid.

"Here," said Declan. "There's an opening."

There was a crack in the wall, just wide enough for a thin person to squeeze through. They shone their torches into it and found a piece of cloth that had stuck to the rough surface.

"That's from Marcus's shirt," said Louisa. "He came through here. It's a tight squeeze, though. Are you game?"

Declan hoped he sounded braver than he felt when he said, "I'll follow you."

They squeezed through the opening, forgetting that they were supposed to stay within earshot of their father.

Declan tried very hard to think about other things. The space was cramped and damp. He could feel one wall scraping the back of his head and the other wall touching his face.

Suddenly the gap opened out. They took a few steps and found themselves in a cave that soared above them and spread before them. Their torches revealed shapes that neither of them had ever seen before. Directly ahead of them, a vast curtain shimmered and glowed. It fell from somewhere far above them and draped itself elegantly in great folds of limestone. It looked as though a breeze might make it curl and flutter, but when Declan reached out his hand and touched its hem it was solid and cold and wet. It had bands running across it at regular intervals and they made it look even more like an enormous piece of cloth that had been stitched together in sections.

Louisa's torch found an arch of stone that dripped stalactites. They were fine and tinted pink. Some of the stalactites looked like straws suspended in space. They ended in points that appeared to be needle sharp. The other stalactites were thicker and their ends were rounded.

Beneath the stalactites, chunky stalagmites rose to meet them.

"Which ones are stalactites?" asked Declan.

"Stalactites have to hold on tight so they won't fall from the roof and stalagmites might one day reach up and touch them," said Louisa. "That's an easy way to remember."

Louisa and Declan, mesmerised by the spectacle in this cavern, forgot for a moment why they were here.

"Marcus!" Louisa called. Her voice ricocheted around the extraordinary formations. There was no answer from Marcus. There was, though, a sudden rustling way up in the ceiling of the cave. It was so far up that their torches didn't throw enough light to see. The rustling grew louder and then settled down.

"What was that?" asked Declan.

"Bats probably," said Louisa. She liked bats. Declan hated bats. Not that he'd ever actually seen a real bat in the wild. He just assumed that he hated them because they looked creepy in the cartoons he had seen.

"They won't hurt you," said Louisa. "There are probably thousands of them up there."

Declan sniffed the air. "It smells like it," he said.

They had been so overwhelmed by what they had seen that they hadn't really paid much attention to what their noses could tell them. Now the smell of the bats was obvious and the torchlight revealed that the cave floor was slick with their droppings.

"What if they fly down here?" said Declan.

"They won't. Besides, I'd like it if they did. There must be lots of weird insects that live in all that muck," Louisa replied.

"Yuck," said Declan.

"Don't worry, I'm not going to look," Louisa assured him. "We have to find Marcus before Dad starts to worry."

They had to move carefully over the surface of this cave because with every step their feet threatened to slide out from under them. One sprained ankle in the family was more than enough.

They kept close to the wall wherever possible, although they frequently had to

go around frozen rock flows that looked like marzipan. On the other side of one of these flows, a long, low structure seemed to seep from the wall. Oozing over it was a deposit of pure white limestone, spread in thick runs like melting wax. Louisa ran her hand over its polished surface.

"Imagine how long this would have taken to form," she said.

"Look at this," said Declan.

He had found a large mud-splash. It looked as if it had been caught and held in a photograph. They could see where a big droplet of water had hit the ground and burst outwards. Incredibly, the shape had been frozen in the mud before it had had a chance to evaporate.

"I wish I had my specimen jar," said Louisa.

Declan came over to her and saw the creature she was observing in the circle of her torchlight. It was completely white. He thought it was creepy and disgusting.

"It's some sort of cricket," said Louisa. "I've read about cave crickets, but I've never seen one."

"It's gross," said Declan.

"It's fascinating," said Louisa. She could never understand why people thought that bugs were disgusting. While she was watching the cricket, Declan walked ahead a little.

"Here's another passage," he said.

Louisa joined him. They discovered

that there were in fact two passages, about eight feet apart.

"Should we split up?" asked Declan. "I wonder which one he went down?"

"No. We can't split up. Dad said not to. Besides, what's the point of finding Marcus and then having to find you."

"Hey," said Declan in an offended voice, "maybe I'd find Marcus and then we'd have to find you."

"Whatever," said Louisa. "We can't split up. We'll just have to take a chance."

Declan was shining his torch back in the direction from which they had come.

"You know, Louisa," he said. "I think we're as lost as Marcus is."

"Rubbish," said Louisa. "We could just go back the way we came."

"Which way was that?" asked Declan.

Louisa shone her torch back along the path they had taken. But everything seemed different. She had been quite sure that retracing their steps would be easy.

But when she looked now, all the formations she had remembered as markers looked unfamiliar, or in the wrong place.

"We could find that opening we came through," she said.

Declan let his torchlight roam across the distant wall. They had thought that there had been one opening. There were dozens and they all looked the same.

"Which one did we come through?" asked Declan.

It might have been fear that made them both alert to the slightest sound, but they were now aware of all sorts of strange noises in the cave. The bats rustled and squeaked and occasionally there was the sound of a falling stone or the dripping of water. There was also a sound like heavy breathing coming from somewhere in the darkness. Declan clutched his sister's arm.

"Is that the madman?" he asked, his voice tight with fear.

"There is no madman. I told you, I made that up just to scare you."

"Well, what is it then?" asked Declan.

The breathing stopped for a moment and then began again. Louisa's imagination created a ferocious and grotesque cave animal unknown to science, waiting to pounce. She shook her head and tried to think coolly and logically. The truth about the noise came to her in a flash.

"It's just the wind, Declan," she said.

"It's the wind forcing its way down a narrow passage."

She was relieved when she said this, because she knew that she was right. When Declan listened again, he too knew that she was right and his terror lifted.

Before deciding which opening to pass through, they examined the ground around each of them. They were hoping to find some evidence that Marcus had passed by here. He might have dropped a handkerchief or a lolly wrapper, or something. There was nothing.

They stood exactly halfway between each opening and concentrated very hard. Louisa knew it was silly, but she thought that if she closed her eyes and formed a picture of Marcus in her mind, she might be drawn like a magnet to the right opening. Declan did the same.

Declan pointed to the left.

Louisa pointed to the right.

In the end, they decided to toss a coin. They headed down the opening on the right. It was just above head height and wide enough for both of them to walk side by side. The floor was flat and dry. Walking was easy.

They would soon discover that it had other perils.

Chapter Five

Lost

The passage ended at a T-intersection. They decided to go right, because it felt like a safe direction. Louisa figured that if they kept going right, then they would just have to keep going left if they had to backtrack.

The new passage suddenly narrowed and they had to crouch to keep going. It then broadened into a space where there were three passages to choose from. They chose the right-hand one, using the same logic as before.

This passage quickly became so narrow that it was impassable. Retracing their steps, they passed through an entrance that they thought was the one they had entered by. But after a few steps, they were overcome by the feeling that it was both familiar and unfamiliar.

"I think we've taken a wrong turn," said Louisa.

"I think we've taken about a dozen wrong turns," said Declan. "We're lost."

When he said this, the awful reality of what this meant hit them both.

"We mustn't panic," said Louisa. "We have to keep calm and think this through. We can't be far from the entrance. We haven't been walking for very long."

She checked her watch and took in a sharp breath of surprise. They had been walking for more than three hours. Their father must be worried sick.

"We have to keep going," she said.

"It doesn't matter what direction we

go in," said Declan. "We don't know any more whether we're going forward or backward."

"We're going forward," said Louisa sternly, as if she could make this true by saying it with enough confidence.

They continued on. The ceiling of this passage got lower and lower. Before long, they had to get down on their stomachs and crawl forward. Declan did not like this. Panic welled up within him.

But they didn't have to crawl very far. Just as Declan thought he couldn't hold his fear in any longer, they came out in another huge chamber. They had to jump from a ledge to enter it.

In the middle of this chamber, water lay still and glassy. It was an unnatural blue and without wind to disturb it, it looked like a sheet of ice. Around the edges of this underground lake were pools of water, lying in terraced sections. When

Declan shone his torch into one of these pools, he saw pearly balls, creamy-white and glossy. He thought they might be the biggest pearls in the world. On one side of the lake, long stalactites hung down in their thousands like strings of snap-frozen rain. The torchlight made them appear both beautiful and eerie.

The sound of dripping water echoed weirdly here, like a thousand taps in a gigantic bathroom. The air temperature had dropped and they both shivered.

Nevertheless, what was spread out before them was so astonishingly beautiful that Declan and Louisa forgot to be afraid.

Suddenly, beyond the lake, Declan and Louisa saw a flash of light that could only have come from Marcus's torch. One moment it was there, then it was gone.

"Marcus!" called Louisa. There was a clatter of rocks as Marcus hurried away.

"Why would he do that?" asked Louisa. "He must know we're all lost."

"What if it isn't Marcus?" asked Declan.

"Who else could it possibly be?" said Louisa, annoyed at Declan for planting a seed of fear in her mind.

"Someone who…"

"Stop it, Declan," Louisa snapped.

Declan's mind was racing and he couldn't stop. "Someone who found Marcus and stole his torch. Or someone else who doesn't want to be found."

Louisa felt her fingers curl and her arms tingle with fear.

"Marcus!" she called. "Stop playing games!"

There was only the echo of her own words for reply.

"If it's Marcus," said Declan, "how did he get across that water?"

"It must be shallow, or maybe he came a different way. It's definitely him, Declan. We've just scared ourselves, that's all. I'm going to see if I can walk through that water."

Louisa was aware that what she was about to do was very dangerous. She had no way of knowing how deep it was, and even if it was shallow, there might be deep holes here and there. If she went slowly, putting one foot in front of the other very carefully, she should be able to feel a hole before falling into it.

"I'll follow," said Declan.

"Okay, but step exactly where I step."

The water was icy cold. As Louisa had suspected, it wasn't deep. About halfway across, the water reached their waists then became shallower as they approached the opposite side.

When Louisa and Declan reached the far side of the lake, they climbed up onto a ledge and found the entrance to a tunnel. Once inside, they could hear the echo of footsteps up ahead. They assumed it was Marcus. Every few feet, they stopped to listen. Marcus's steps could still be heard.

But when they stopped for the fifth time, they could no longer hear him. They strained to hear the footsteps. Nothing. Then an altogether different sound reached them, a low rumble. And there was something else as well—the unmistakable sound of rushing water.

It began as a trickle, but soon water was rushing over their feet. The torch-light showed that it was racing through the tunnel. They could hear it spilling out into the lake behind them. They hurried forward. The water rose steadily and its flow tugged at their clothes and almost swept them off their feet. The noise was incredible. Deafening.

Keeping their torches clear of the water, they struggled to move on. The tunnel was filling rapidly. Soon it would be over their heads and they would not be able to swim against it. They would be picked up and carried along like twigs before being thrown into the glassy lake.

If they could have seen the lake now, they would not have recognised it. The water churned and frothed as it received the rush from the tunnel.

Louisa grabbed Declan's hand.

"We won't let go of each other!" she yelled. "We'll get out of this, I promise!"

Declan nodded. He was more afraid than he had ever been in his life, but he knew that, for both their sakes, he must not show it. He gripped Louisa's hand until his nails dug into her palms.

"Up here! Up here!"

Marcus's voice could just be heard above the din of the pounding water. Louisa found him, crouched on a ledge. The water had reached their chests now and was splashing into their mouths. They had to move quickly. Marcus leaned over and offered his hand. Louisa pushed Declan forward and lifted him while Marcus dragged him clear. Then Louisa, with Marcus and Declan pulling her up, clambered to temporary safety.

Louisa wanted to shake Marcus and shout at him. But, when she shone her torch into his face, he didn't look like the defiant, cheeky Marcus she knew. It was the face of a frightened boy—a boy who knew that he had gone too far; this time he had led his cousins into a place they might never escape from. His skin was pale, he was shivering with cold and his eyes were red with tears.

"We can find a way out," said Louisa.

"If we stick together, we'll be fine."

Marcus shivered. "I was just exploring," he said, lamely.

The water was still rising and moving more and more rapidly. If one of them fell into it now, there would be no hope of rescue. It was swirling with foam.

Louisa raked the walls above her with her torch. There was a black hole about two metres up which was probably a tunnel. There were also outcrops of rock which would act as steps.

They would have to be very careful. One slip and they would be pitched into what had now become a raging underground river. She indicated to the two boys that this was where they had to go. She went first, making sure that the rocks were solid. One of them was loose and tumbled into the flood.

Once beyond the lip of this opening, she shone her torch on each of the stones that were secure. Marcus went up next, placing his feet where the light was. Declan followed close behind.

This tunnel was dry and the roar of the water was muffled. They could speak to each other without shouting.

"I was just exploring," said Marcus again. But even he knew how silly his words sounded.

Louisa sat down, exhausted.

"We've been away for hours," she said. "Dad will be frantic." Louisa felt like crying. Instead, she stood up and looked at the boys. "We'll have to keep going," she said.

Declan turned his head sharply to one side. "What was that?" he said.

"What?"

"Shhh!"

They all listened intently. Very faintly, they heard someone calling.

Louisa cupped her hands and shouted with all her might.

"We're here! We're here!"

With renewed energy, they headed down the tunnel towards the calling. As they got closer, they could hear quite clearly Mr Mackenzie's voice.

"Louisa! Declan!"

"We're here!" they shouted in return. They then heard what sounded like a whoop of joy.

The tunnel they were walking in twisted and turned, but it did not split into different passages. Incredibly, it led directly back to the main entrance of the cave. When they emerged into the main chamber, they could see the light where they had first come in and they could see the silhouette of Mr Mackenzie against it.

"We're here!" yelled Louisa for the umpteenth time and she laughed with relief. They were safe. The children hugged each other, aware of how close they had come to being lost forever.

Louisa and Declan rushed to their father and clung tightly to him. On Mr Mackenzie's face, relief struggled with anger, but relief won and he hugged them both.

Marcus held back.

Chapter Six

On the Road

The rain had stopped, but the ground outside the cave had turned into a sort of sticky mousse. Mr Mackenzie's ankle was still painful, but some of the swelling had gone. The bruise had spread though. He assured the children that it looked far worse than it felt.

Nevertheless, getting Mr Mackenzie from the cave back to the camp site was a struggle. It took all three of them to help him hobble over the slippery ground. He tried not to put too much weight on them, although Marcus imagined he leaned a little too heavily on him.

When they reached the camp site, they found it badly damaged. Mr Mackenzie's tent was lying under a very large branch.

"Lucky we went to the cave," said Marcus, hoping his uncle's escape from being crushed might cool his temper.

"Yes," said Mr Mackenzie slowly. "We've all been very lucky."

Louisa, Declan and Marcus were soaked through and spattered with mud. They were shivering with cold. They couldn't light a fire. All the kindling was saturated. Mr Mackenzie ordered them into the car. Hopping on his good leg, he got towels out of the boot and a change of clothes for all of them. Then he turned on the engine and put the car's heater on high. They were soon warm. They were also now calm enough to think about all that had happened in the last few hours.

Mr Mackenzie sat in the driver's seat, tapping on the steering wheel with his fingers. Marcus sat on the seat next to him. From the back seat, Louisa could see her father's eyes in the rear-view mirror. He was frowning, but his eyes did not look angry. She could tell when he was angry. He was puzzled, perhaps. No, it wasn't that, either. She couldn't read his emotion. This was something she hadn't seen before.

Declan was bursting to tell his father about the fabulous things he had seen. Now that he was no longer in danger, he wanted to share his adventure. He was about to speak when Louisa silenced him by punching him gently on the leg.

"What?" he said automatically.

"Later," she whispered.

Mr Mackenzie turned to his children. "I want you to tell me everything that happened in the cave," he said.

"But first I want to say that I blame myself and that I am not angry with you. I'm not even angry with you Marcus. I should never have let you explore that cave. I can't believe that I was so foolish."

"No, Dad," said Louisa. "It would have been all right if we'd done what you told us to do."

"That's not the point," he said. "I knew what Marcus was like. There was every chance that he would wander off and I still let you explore. I have to take responsibility for that." He paused.

"There's something else, too. Last night, I didn't get much sleep. My ankle was very painful and I just couldn't fall asleep. Not long after you went off exploring the cave, I fell asleep. I must have slept for a few hours. When I woke up and realised what had happened, I didn't know what to do. I called and called and called. You have no idea how relieved I was when I heard you answer."

"You have no idea how relieved we were to hear you," said Louisa.

"You weren't in any real danger, were you?" asked Mr Mackenzie.

"No," Louisa answered quickly. "No. We were just exploring."

Marcus looked at his cousin. If he'd had a million dollars he would have given it to her at that moment. In a silent communication they agreed that there were some things Mr Mackenzie didn't need to know.

Declan began an excited description of the world within the cave. His father listened and thought he was probably exaggerating, especially when Declan described the bats. But Louisa confirmed all that he said.

"It sounds like you've had quite an experience. Are you sure you were safe at all times?" Mr Mackenzie suspected that Declan was holding back. For example, why were they so wet, and why were they so pleased to see him?

"What did you mean when you said it would have been all right if you'd obeyed my instructions?" Mr Mackenzie asked Louisa.

Louisa thought for a moment. How could she answer her father without telling a lie?

"I just meant that you wouldn't have been worried and we wouldn't have got a bit lost. I admit we did get a bit lost and it wasn't much fun."

"That was my fault," said Marcus. "I wandered off. I'm sorry Uncle John."

This was a world-first. Marcus had never apologised for anything in his life.

"Well," said Mr Mackenzie, slightly taken aback. "You were right about the tent. If we hadn't gone to the cave, I might have been in there when the branch fell on it."

Louisa, Declan and Marcus cleaned up the camp site and packed up the tents.

They collected their belongings and put them in the boot of the car. They made sure there was no rubbish left behind.

"Are you ready yet?" called Mr Mackenzie.

Louisa and Declan got into the car.

"Where's Marcus, now?" said Mr Mackenzie. He wound down his window and shouted, "Marcus!"

There was no answer.

"I don't believe this," he said.